40 days to a Joyful Motherhood

by Sarah Humphrey

Illustrations by Emily Little

DEXTERITY
NASHVILLE

604 Magnolia Lane
Nashville, TN 37211

Printed in the United States of America.

First edition: 2023 0 9 8 7 6 5 4 3 2 1

ISBN: 978-1-947297-62-3
ISBN: 978-1-947297-63-0 (E-book)

Publisher's Cataloging-in-Publication Data

Names: Humphrey, Sarah, 1981-, author. | Little, Emily, 1972-, illustrator.
Title: 40 days to a joyful motherhood / by Sarah Humphrey; illustrated by Emily Little.
Description: Nashville, TN: Dexterity, 2023.
Identifiers: ISBN 978-1-947297-62-3 (paperback) | 978-1-947297-63-0 (ebook)
Subjects: LCSH Motherhood. | Motherhood--Religious aspects--Christianity. | Devotional calendars. | Mothers--Prayers and devotions. | BISAC RELIGION / Christian Living / Devotional Journal | RELIGION / Christian Living / Parenting
Classification: LCC BV4529.18 .H86 2023 | DDC 242/.6431--dc23

Book design by Sarah Siegand
Cover photo/illustrations by Emily Little

Dedicated to my first loves:

David, Ella, (Micah), Lucy, and Oliver.

And to all the women in the world
who rejoice in the title of "mom."

Contents

Foreword

New moms and seasoned moms alike all strive to be good mothers. Whether we are working moms, stay-at-home moms, or single moms, it is our natural and God-given instinct to care for, nurture, and love our children with our whole hearts. In the morning, we think of them and prepare what they need for their days. During the day, we pray for them, feed them, teach them, comfort them, and guide them. In the evening, we tuck them in, kiss them good night, and thank God for them.

In a day and age where mothering comes with a myriad of choices, a lot of pressure, and sometimes quite a few complications, women need encouragement. Parenting is both the hardest job we'll ever have and also the most rewarding. Wanting what's best for our kids is not enough to actually *give* them what's best. It's the in-between grit and details that make our lives as mothers reality.

In *40 Days to a Joyful Motherhood*, Sarah helps us with just that. She provides Scripture references, emotional tools, and simple prayers to guide and encourage her readers in their mothering journeys. Each day is hearty enough to invite deep connection to God, prayer, and peace but also brief enough to meet a busy mom right where she is, simply for fifteen minutes. Maybe you don't have an hour or two a day to sit down and read, but I guarantee you have time to rest and relish in these daily devotions. They will not only enlighten your day with purpose, joy, and hope, but they will encourage, empower, and meet you where you are in the thick of your motherhood.

Delightfully funny, vulnerably honest, and doing the very work herself, Sarah shows us that mothering is not about perfection and performance, but about the very heart of God. It's in His heart for us that we can be the best mothers for our kids. We are chosen by God Himself, and He knows how many hairs are on our heads, how much responsibility we carry, and how sincerely we want to enjoy our children. It is in His care for us that we grow in our nurturing and peace as moms.

As Sarah dives into topics of identity, self-care, grief, boundaries, presence, and forgiveness, you will engage with yourself as a person and as a mother. Seeing how our lives as women and mothers intertwine is sprinkled all through her devotions, and it models the connected life that God has offered to us in parenthood. What I hope you gain from this reading experience is not only a personal journey into the practical side of motherhood, but also a deeper look into your soul as a woman. When motherhood comes, it can seem as though all other pieces of our lives take on a new shape, and that is true. Mothering changes everything. But what Sarah's book shows us all is that mothering enhances and enlivens the lives we already have, and it also heals, nurtures, and embraces the parts of our hearts that we may not have yet cared for. In a mix of healing, laughter, and emotional transformation, Sarah describes the process of mothering with intention, discovery, care, and hope. Most mothers deal with depression or anxiety in some regard; they seem to be part of the process. And though they can take a toll, they can also bring new life and peace to every place in our hearts and bodies that needs it. This book will guide you in just that!

As a mother of three, I cherish moments with my children. Whether I am on the road with *Inside Edition*, creating television shows for Christmas, or writing books of my own, my greatest inspiration comes from home, where my husband and kids light up my life. And having a book like *40 Days to a Joyful Motherhood* traveling with me on the airplanes, in a taxi, or while snuggled up on my couch brings me such joy, peace, and encouragement.

I know you'll delight in these pages as much as I did and do. You will find rest, hope, instruction, guidance, and a friend. Sarah's journey will influence yours in a way that makes mothering not only a gift but a calling. Let her meet you in the details, let God's spirit inspire you through the words, and relish in the fact that you are doing a great job! You wouldn't have picked this book up if you weren't.

Enjoy the journey, and engage in her prayer prompts and practical activation. Allow God to bring nourishment into your heart and energy to your soul. Mothers make the world go round, and it's a joy to be in these pages embracing it all!

Megan Alexander

Author of *Faith in the Spotlight, One More Hug,*
and *The Magic of a Small Town Christmas*;
National correspondent at CBS/Paramount Entertainment
and host of UPtv's *Small Town Christmas*

Welcome

Every mother can relate with one common theme during her pregnancy, childbirth, adoption process, first days of parenting, and beyond: the need for joy.

What makes us most effective as birthers and nurturers, as boundary makers and guidance counselors, is joy. When we speak from a posture of abundance and life, we fill our surroundings with peace and purpose. When we live out of exhaustion, fear, and depression, we deplete the very place we are supposed to steward. As mothers, we face both of these situations at different times. It is inevitable. Motherhood is full of trial and error, leadership and development, unconditional love, and mistakes. Yet, in the vast array of emotions and experiences, we can learn how to cultivate a home full of honor. As we face ourselves and hand ourselves over to Jesus to be healed, loved, and filled up, we can then create an environment where we give our families and friends the space to do the same.

What every mother wants is to be happy and healthy. What I've developed out of my own journey of motherhood is a tool just for that. Out of my ups and downs, I'm learning how to pray. I'm also learning how to look at myself deeply, how to live life simply, and how to give practically. My hope through this project is that it might give you insight and tools on how to do the same in your own unique experience.

So let's talk about it. Let's talk about the perfect, but sometimes does not feel so perfect, *storm.*

Hormones. No sleep. Body parts that are all kinds of sizes they weren't before. Skin that's flabby and swollen and creating muffin tops that make the world go round.

Emotions of love and joy and excitement and "Oh God, please don't cry again."

And if you are blessed, multiple children who simultaneously do not understand how your body and personhood just went through a hurricane and is somehow holding on with one thread of dignity and a side of hemorrhoid cream.

Yeah, I said it.

Welcome to childbirth and motherhood! These are the days when biological mothers have no idea where all that milk came from and wonder how their bodies became the creative source to keep a human being alive. Adoptive mothers may meet this day with both overflowing fear and joy, where expectations have become reality, where what has been hoped for is now in full throttle, and whom you've prayed for is right in front of you!

It is amazing, really, and it is full of curiosity and expectation and learning and growing.

It is also full of what feels like "not enough time" though "not enough time" is really just a shift of priorities, even if it doesn't always feel like that in the moment.

My biggest shift in parenting bliss was learning how to process everything that was happening with a sense of peace and joy. In the midst of daily life, moms are constantly trying to listen, troubleshoot, and respond to needs, all without many avenues for self-care. And this, in fact, is the most crucial time in life for self-care—not just as a person, but for the role of motherhood.

When I decided to be a stay-at-home mom, my greatest asset was using motherhood as a time to relearn nurture, both as a mother and for myself. Bringing a baby into the world is also a season of bringing new creativity, new life, and new gifts to our homes and to the world.

Motherhood is also a time of relearning and regrowing; it is a time of exposure. It is a season in which many of the unnurtured parts of us start to show up quite loudly, and so it is also a time of healing and repair.

The tricky part that young moms always go back to is my first case and point: there is not much personal time. A newborn is the center of attention, and if other children are involved, personal time is limited. What I learned to do, and am still learning to do, is make the most of the time I do have for myself. I had to shift priorities and learn how to manage all the emotions and inspiration and creativity of my being and then funnel them into something productive and life-giving to me. I had to give myself time for release. Because if I did not give myself room for creative release, I would end up spewing emotional outbursts onto someone else which is usually hurried, frustrating, and potentially hurtful.

I am not usually a formula-type person. I am more of a go-with-the-flow person, but sometimes my flow ends up creating a pattern. Ironically, that pattern gives me wisdom on how to do well the next time. In hope that my pattern will be encouraging to you, here is my motherhood story.

Let joy be our portion!

Identity

My husband has worked in the publishing industry for over twelve years, and he says the books that sell the quickest off the shelves are the ones with the most blunt titles. In other words: *5 Steps to Be Happy* or *How to Deal with Anxiety* or *Hi, I Just Had Three Kids and Am Trying to Make Sense of My Crazy Self*. You get the idea.

When it came to having kids and naming them, we first went with what sounded good (because we love beautiful names), but we also went with what had deep meaning to us as a married couple. And simply enough, the names of our kids have represented those characteristics and traits in many blunt and beautiful ways through our daily lives. Experiencing that has given me wisdom while walking through not only this particular season with them, but hopefully their entire lives.

Our Ella is the female version of "Who is like God?" She teaches me how to listen and how to move. Our Lucy is "Light." She teaches me about self-care and healthy boundaries. Our Oliver is "Peace and fruitfulness." He teaches me to regain laughter and strength.

As a writer, it's sometimes easy to think of each child as a book (we are all the authors of our stories, yes?), and their names are the blunt titles I remind myself of when I'm trying to figure out how to raise them as well as grow personally.

If I have clung to one thing during this season of life, it has been to move toward what their names and their identities mean. Children are God's gifts to us, so my "gifts" are God's representation of women, His light, and His peace. These are my personal keys. When all else seems overwhelming with dirty diapers and crying and temper tantrums, I go back to these keys. These are the purposes that God is having me steward in myself, in my marriage, and in each one of them. These are the gifts that have been given as a result of love between David and me; these define who we are as a family and illustrate what we value. When I can see the big picture, it is easier to let the small and overly complicated details work themselves out. Because as moms, we obsess over the details while parenting all the time: Is my kid nursing well? Is my kid going to learn how to talk? Is my kid eating enough healthy food? Is my kid sleeping through the night? And on and on and on. It is the details that start to kill our energy and our joy and our peace. The details begin to make us compare ourselves to one another and start mommy wars. The details make us perfectionists who are hard on ourselves for every small, minute issue that goes awry (which happens more when that's what we are focusing on).

So, instead of perfectionism, I chose to move toward meaning, which gave me the wisdom to sort out the details well.

I chose to focus on identity. I decided to move toward God's beauty for women, His light, and His peace, because those are our kids. As I focused on this, the opposites showed up often (because there is an opponent for every good choice), but I knew my purpose. So, as the opposites reared their ugly heads, I just reminded myself of what I had birthed. Those beautiful human beings with those identities came out of my womb. I decided I was going to continue moving toward God's beauty for women, His light, and His peace with all my might while also honoring the challenges and feelings that surfaced in my heart. This was quite a number of cycles, and still can be. But people (including mothers) are onions: we have a lot of layers. We have unresolved hurts, experiences, and generational lines of good and hard experiences that have mixed their way into our DNA—and it can take a lot of focus and hard work to rewire ourselves.

Because in all reality, our struggles in motherhood and our challenges within ourselves are what make us grow and learn. Those mishaps in our generational or personal wiring become obvious to us when we are faced with seeing them in our circumstances and in our children. Those mishaps showed me where to close the gaps in my life so I could be happier and more effective as a person and wife and mother.

My first round of encouragement to the mamas of today is this: find out what your kids' names mean. Sit down and ask yourself what they represent to you. And when the opposite of that starts to reveal itself (because it will), face it eye to eye. Honor the emotions that the opposition brings up, and keep moving toward the reconciliation.

Because as we move toward the reconciliation, our faith ripens and our fears disappear. When that fear starts to disappear, we start to actually settle into our motherhood with a profound sense of peace and joy. And what our children need most from us as mothers is just that.

Day 1

I will make of you a great nation and will bless you.
I will make your name respected, and you will be a blessing.

Genesis 12:2 CEB

As we embark on the journey of motherhood and reflect on the names of our children, we also need to remember our identity as a person is of utmost significance. We can't fully provide for our kids unless we are nourished ourselves. So, today is about us. *Who are you?* What is your name? What is the meaning of your name? Who you are is important, and it is vital to your success as a person, as a wife, as a mother, and as a friend. Often, we put ourselves on the back burner when we realize that our children need our attention twenty-four hours of the day and seven days of the week. In the midst of these needs, God knows who we are. Today is a day to remember how He named us.

Let's focus on our names. Write down your full name. If you don't know the meaning of your name, Google it. Find out why you were given your particular name. Listen to your birth story. Invite yourself to recalibrate all the life experiences, good and bad, that make up you and your life. This is a time of rebirth. Even as you have birthed or adopted a child, you are also birthing a new version of yourself!

A Simple Prayer

Jesus, let me learn more about who I am. I open my heart to

hear You speak into the identity

You have created for me.

Day 2

Adorn yourself with splendor and majesty;
clothe yourself with honor and esteem.

Job 40:10 CEB

What fills your love tank? How do you refuel? Think big or small, simple or complex. Acts of self-care and self-love are extremely important to mothers. Filling up before giving out is essential to living life well and giving with joy. What we fail to give ourselves, we fail to release to others.

Before I was a mother, I had an extreme addiction to giving too much. I am a giver by nature and love to help others, but without understanding boundaries in a proper context, it was easy for me to serve more than my mind and body could handle. When I became a mother, it forced me to look at myself—at the way I thought, ate, and exercised as well as the way I spent my time and energy. It rewired my whole system of doing things in every way imaginable. It saved my life in many ways.

The transition to motherhood is very abrupt because a baby takes up every hour of every day (and night). And so, with this new life, I learned how to take cover and take care. I learned how to set healthy limits (it's OK to say no!) and how to open myself to God's love, self-love, and friends who cared. I read my Bible more, prayed more, and put better boundaries on my time. I reminded myself of joy with simple things and big things: a cup of coffee, an hour of quiet, a trip with girlfriends, journaling, and art. What I wanted to do on a regular basis was to be kind to myself.

Find ways today to look for simple joys. Come back to this entry later and write down a few of the kind things you did for yourself today. Spend time looking at your actions today and how you took care of yourself.

A Simple Prayer

Jesus, help me to fill my love tank first.
Please give me practical tips on how
to take good care of myself.

Day 3

Anyone who needs wisdom should ask God,
whose very nature is to give to everyone
without a second thought, without keeping score.
Wisdom will certainly be given to those who ask.

James 1:5 CEB

Becoming self-aware is one of our greatest personal tools. Recognizing areas where we struggle or where we overextend ourselves is the key to creating proper balance and boundaries in our lives. After we create an environment of self-care, it is good to pay attention to where we get off-kilter, overemotional, or irritated. These are signals to us to listen to ourselves, to let go of difficult emotions, and to choose a revised path. When I feel depleted or anxious, I realize that I have inside work to do. A struggle is actually the path to greatness. Whether it is lack of sleep, my child's health, or any other experience in life, I can face any difficulty by practicing self-awareness, releasing toxicity, allowing God to touch my heart, setting good boundaries, and re-creating joy.

The best way to come to a healthy version of ourselves is to release toxicity from our lives. Sometimes that is putting a boundary on a relationship, on extra activities, or on other stressors that create an environment in which we fail to thrive. When we give ourselves space to be the best versions of ourselves, we can let go of the things that hinder us.

What are some boundaries in your life that need to be drawn? What are some toxins you would like to release? What are some emotions you need to process and let go of? This could be as small as forgiving yourself for leaving the dishes undone or as big as giving God the room in your heart to work in a deep way. Sometimes motherhood joy is as simple as getting a good night's sleep, but other times it can be healing a canyon of unexpressed feelings and hurts, old addictions, or childhood wounds. Wherever you are in your journey, God is there with you.

A Simple Prayer

Jesus, help me to become self-aware. Please give me wisdom and guidance to know my boundaries and to be honest with my emotions.

Day 4

On the day I cried out, you answered me.
You encouraged me with inner strength.

Psalm 138:3 CEB

A fter we've brought ourselves into a posture of peace and joy, we can then give from the resulting outflow to our family. Just as we need to be reminded of our own identity, so do our loved ones. If you are married, what is the name of your husband? What does his name mean? What are the names of your children? What do those names mean?

It is important to find the meaning of their names because this will show us how to encourage them, build them up, and feed them with the best soul food. As mothers, we call our family members *up* to their identity, and we put boundaries on what hinders those identities. When we recognize the opposite spirit rising against who they are, we remind them of truth.

This is always the key. We never want to shame or point blame; we always want to call them higher, nurture, and then set a guideline for better behavior.

We are better wives when we call our husbands up to their potential instead of nag about their weaknesses. We steward greatness, safety, and peace in our children when we give out both encouragement and wisdom.

Moms are often most vulnerable to imbalance because of the many demands on their time and resources. When we speak from a place of identity in ourselves to a place of identity in our loved ones, we create balance so our family can thrive.

Write down the meaning behind the names of your husband and children. Also, write down the opposites of their names so that you are aware of what they might need to overcome obstacles in their lives.

A Simple Prayer

*Jesus, please help me to encourage the identity
and potential in those I love. Give me eyes to see them
the way You see them.*

Day 5

Do not conform to the pattern of this world, but be transformed by the renewing of your mind. Then you will be able to test and approve what God's will is—his good, pleasing and perfect will.

Romans 12:2 NIV

Transformation is the key to living a joyful life. When we are able to recognize and interrupt broken patterns in our lives and in the lives of our children, we learn the essence of forgiveness. And in forgiveness, we learn the proper way to steward. I want to steward joy in my home. In order to do that, I realize a few practical steps go a long way.

My first step is to honor original design. God says He created us and we are good. This has to be my standard for identity, then! It is also obvious that we all have and will, at times, fall short of this original design. Out of His good grace, God gave us Jesus. It is in this place of surrender, humility, and brokenness that we can receive God's grace. When we have given Him those weak and fragile parts, the mistakes and the failures, the bad behavior and the sin, we experience His gift toward us. In the gift of Jesus, we are filled with the joy and peace needed to start making better decisions. And with our good decisions comes transformation.

Personally, this transformation gives me strength for myself, and it releases the essence of true motherhood through me. Good mothers honor design, they understand sin, they ask for forgiveness, they fill up with joy, and they make better decisions for the future. We all begin here, and it is never too late to start on this path. Whether you are a mother to be, a new mother, or have been a mother for a long time, we rely on this cycle. Transformation is the beauty of life. Understanding and promoting this cycle is what makes us mothers.

Think about what you shared on Day 1 as the meaning of your name; this is your original design. Day 2 shared ways you can help honor that design. Day 3 discussed ways we have fallen short or areas in which we need healing. Day 4 is who we primarily share that healing with and who we help steward. Today, let's ask for transformation in this cycle. Thank God for goodness and for who you are, and acknowledge where you need to go. Apologize for where you went wrong, and offer up a healing transformation so that you can give well to yourself and to your family. Take some time to pray and be with God inside this cycle.

A Simple Prayer

Jesus, transform me. Please give me the tools to steward my life and the life of my children in a meaningful and joyful way.

Pain, Progress, & Prayer

The greatest gift in my life as a person, a wife, a mother, and a friend is prayer. C. S. Lewis says, "Pain insists upon being attended to. God whispers to us in our pleasures, speaks in our consciences, but shouts in our pains. It is his megaphone to rouse a deaf world." As a human being, it is inevitable that you know pain.

If you have ever birthed a child, you know pain. If you have ever carried a friend's burden, you know pain. If you have ever had a loved one pass from this life, you know pain. If you have ever really lived, you know pain.

Pain is often part of our lives. Not always, but often. Unfortunately, much of the population has not been given many tools to understand it. We find myriad "treatments" to numb it, pill pop it, pass by it, or drink it down. This is a detriment to our culture, our children, our families, and our livelihoods. Sadly, it can be difficult for young mothers to find good outlets for all the feelings they are experiencing.

Since my oldest was born, I have been on a journey to process my feelings and express them more clearly. This has taught me how to heal my personal pain, learn to pray, and also how to make progress as a woman and caregiver. I grew up in a blended family with as much commitment as there was dysfunction. We didn't have a lot of emotional tools to help us decode all that we experienced, and no one in my family seemed to have it easy. Every life was wrought with some sort of distinct challenge or difficulty. We were tender and broken, but also strong-willed and trying our best. Looking back, I not only learned through our hardships, but I also became a better person. It took time, but the healing happened faithfully and through God's perfect will for all of us.

As mothers raising our own families, we are almost always in the role of teacher, nurse, or counselor. It is simply the way of life. And while we are dealing with our own feelings and struggles—whether that is physical from childbirth, mental from old wounds or hurts, or spiritual from a change in priorities. We have the opportunity to work through things that cause us challenge. Sometimes, it's downright funny and we can laugh. For instance, how in the world can we be wearing an adult diaper for a month postpartum? Maybe someone should start a business for "mommy and me" diapers; it could be a trend! But other times, it is not humorous like diapers or leaking body parts; sometimes it is deep like an ocean of sadness that has never been touched by light.

The family unit was designed by God to be a community of support. As mothers, our opportunity is to create the life environment where everyone can thrive. This can feel like a lot of responsibility. The reality is that many mothers come from histories that may be less than stellar. Sometimes we grew up in dysfunction, sometimes we made our own dysfunction, and sometimes we encounter seasons that are just difficult. Mothering while healing is a lifelong journey for most.

The interesting part of this process is that everyone has her own unique storyline. This means that my path might not look like another person's path, and that is OK. And while social media and Googling have helped us in some small ways to find practical answers for new-mom questions about how to store breast milk or make homemade baby food, it has also created a disconnect in terms of our expectations of daily life. Most of us are not supermodels, chefs, or Instagram influencers; we are simply trying to raise human beings with the best tools we have from the way we were raised. And in our moments of failure, mom guilt, or shame, my hope is that we can move toward prayer and progress over any type of perfectionism and performance.

What we need is God and grace. And you know what? We also might need mercy too. That is OK. Because where we have come from and where we are going are deeply intertwined with our now. That is where our pain can meet healing, that is where our prayers turn into praise, and that is where our hearts turn from sorrow to joy.

Day 6

"For I know the plans I have for you," declares the LORD,
"plans to prosper you and not to harm you,
plans to give you hope and a future."

Jeremiah 29:11 NIV

It is easy to celebrate life when God exceeds our expectations. Sometimes we hold really high expectations in an effort to keep ourselves hopeful or full of faith. Other times we keep low expectations because we have been disappointed and are scared to hope. And sometimes our expectations are simply just ideas, perhaps what we would like to happen. We might not hold on too tightly or loosely, but they are guides for us. No matter what we expect, motherhood comes with hopes and dreams, pains and prayers. When our expectations are exceeded or met, we often feel a sense of satisfaction or connection with life, our surroundings, and others. If our expectations are not met or are dramatically different, sometimes it takes some time emotionally to absorb the differences. Motherhood is an array of hopes and dreams, and we cannot predict very much of it. What we can do is learn how to process that anticipation in a flexible way that can be molded and shaped for the release God intends for us.

What expectations did you have of motherhood before becoming a mother? How did they turn out? I expected it to be easier than it was; I didn't know that my days would feel so long and sometimes lonely. What are some of your hopes, struggles, and prayers as a person? What are some of your hopes, struggles, and prayers as a mother? I hoped life would be calm, connected, and slow. That was not often the case, and so I prayed through struggles of anxiety, worked through fear, and gained a clearer picture of God's love for me. And if you are yet to be a mother, what are some expectations you have for motherhood? What feelings do you have about the uncertainty that lies ahead? Faith or fear? Confidence or concern? Write them all down in a way that expresses your heart.

A Simple Prayer

Jesus, help me to celebrate when You have exceeded my expectations. Guide my expectations of motherhood into a healthy funnel for prayer and release.

Day 7

I give thanks to you with all my heart, LORD. I sing your praise before all other gods. I bow toward your holy temple and thank your name for your loyal love and faithfulness because you have made your name and word greater than everything else. On the day I cried out, you answered me. You encouraged me with inner strength.

Psalm 138:1–3 CEB

Gratitude is a key component to mental health as a person and as a mother. When our days have been met with grace and excitement, we feel full. We feel like all is right with the world, and we are postured in a place of celebration. We meet our children with joy, and the world is our oyster. We live from the very fiber of our beings. When our prayers come true, it is important to take note and give thanks. Gratitude heals our minds and bodies of hope deferred, of disappointment, and of depression. Giving thanks not only releases praise, but it also shifts the mood of our home and environments. I want to spend my life being grateful for how I have been blessed. I want to give praise where I have seen God provide for me, where I have seen dreams come true, and where I have seen faithfulness. Giving thanks is a simple gesture that moves mountains. When I re-member how to be grateful, I open myself up to the possibility of even more blessings.

What are some of the ways you have seen your pain turn into praise? What are some of the simple joys in your life for which you can give thanks, personally and as a mother? Think big and small. Keep an ongoing journal or list of things for which you are thankful. You can always go back to this list when you need a reminder, and you can watch it grow as you continue to pray through struggles and give credit for blessings.

A Simple Prayer

Jesus, thank You for my life's simple joys.

Thank You for continually blessing me.

Remind me to stay alive in gratitude.

Day 8

And we know that in all things God works for the good of those who love Him, who have been called according to His purpose.

Romans 8:28 NIV

Sometimes we hold goals so high or make them so lofty that they are extremely difficult to attain, especially if they deal with another human being. One of the most wonderful things about God is that He is better than any goal we could have, especially when it relates to being a parent. He will always come through, always be faithful, and always be kind. Sometimes He positions us in a way that our human expectations fail so that He can fill us with the truth and the goodness of who He is. And in that, every true hope we could ever have is met.

The reality, though, is that we often have disappointments in the human world that show up without knocking. And when that happens, we work through some pain. I repeatedly felt this when my kids turned out to be introverts when I was used to being an extrovert. There were several years when I thought I would never not be nursing, holding a baby, or be able to drop them off at school without tears. I wondered when I would ever have spare time not to have a person hanging off my person. I felt overstimulated and tired. I watched other mothers drop their kids off with ease, and I wondered if I would ever belong to myself again. And this is where I learned the art of grief.

When we hope for something and the seemingly opposite happens or our plans for a situation are not met, there is a time for legitimate sadness. It is important to note these instances because they often repeat in cycles throughout our lives. Being honest and grieving when what we hoped would happen does not is actually healthy, and putting those plans in God's hands gives Him space to heal us perfectly while weaving His true plan into action.

What are some areas as a person and as a mother where you might have struggled with disappointment? Have you had goals in your parenting that ended up teaching you how to grieve instead of resulting in success?

A Simple Prayer

Jesus, help me not to be stilted by disappointments that turned out differently than I had hoped. Help me to give You my heart in exchange for true fulfillment.

Day 9

Yes, goodness and faithful love will pursue me all the days of my life,
and I will live in the LORD's house as long as I live.

Psalm 23:6 CEB

After we start to understand cycles in our lives when our expectations seem to be unmet and then grieve in response, we open ourselves up to other possibilities. When we make this sacred space in our heart to be honest with ourselves and to be honest with God, we can learn how to take ownership in our healing, admit our mistakes, and release any negative emotions hindering our progress. We can also start to choose new patterns for our lives; we can create new strategies.

My personal preference for growth is that it is slow and steady. If I can make simple changes, one step at a time, I continually see improvement. A willing spirit combined with simple and practical changes can shift pain into a tree of life. I remembered this many times when my children were first starting to homeschool. Of course, I had plans for our school days and what the outcomes would look like. When we had days that focused more on sibling squabbles instead of reading books, I could start to reel into a cycle of defeat. But when I let go of my need to succeed, I often let out a few tears and then noticed that restoring a sibling squabble in a healthy way was just as important as reading comprehension. In many ways, they actually went hand in hand. What I thought was a failure was really just another expression of where we could experience victory.

What are some simple ways you can reframe your "failures"? How can you change habits that have been hindering you? Can you rearrange your schedule or clear out some clutter? Perhaps start each day with a clean kitchen or simply go to bed at a decent hour. How can you incorporate fifteen minutes a day of quiet and prayer into your life? Do you have a safe friend or two you can ask for support in your journey? Think through a few small steps that may make a big difference.

A Simple Prayer

Jesus, please give me the grace to make positive changes that can affect my whole day. Help me to find quiet time to pray daily and create new patterns for my life.

Day 10

Let your gentleness show in your treatment of all people.
The LORD is near.

Philippians 4:5 CEB

After we redirect some of our past disappointments or reorganize some of our new priorities, it is also important to make proper boundaries so we can continue to move forward. Sometimes we have to leave behind old triggers or toxic relationships if we are to bloom with grace. Other times, we just need to let go of old patterns that set us up for frustration. When we start moving forward with focus and clarity, with our expectations fully set on God, we have the strength to let go of hindrances. When we find fresh purpose in our mothering, we can give up what entangles us. Sometimes that is through repetitive practice or simply from choosing to leave behind the old and build the new.

This is the season when we learn the art of gentleness, of being kind to ourselves as we shift patterns and learn new ways to hope and dream. Motherhood comes with many surprises, and sometimes the key to grace is simply being open to what is presented to us. Though children do not come with owner's manuals, we can listen to the Holy Spirit for guidance. We can pray, and we can become quiet in our souls. We can respond to God's leading in order to let go of where we are hindered. God's plans for us are always better than we could have expected or dreamed for ourselves. Our position is childlike faith, releasing false beliefs, and moving toward His perfect heart for us.

As we continue to learn how to be kind to ourselves by making these small shifts each day, we begin to receive God's plans for us in a whole new way. When I look at my children and watch them learn to walk or read, I am always cheering! When God watches us in our everyday lives, He is cheering us on as well. Sometimes that can be difficult to remember when we've had several tough days. No matter the situation, though, He is always on our side and walking with us in gentleness.

What are some areas where you want to see freedom grow in your life? What are some hindrances you want to let go of? What are some simple ways you can promote self-care and gentleness in your day as you transition from old cycles of defeat into fresh trails of freedom?

A Simple Prayer

Jesus, help me to move in the right direction and create the proper boundaries for myself. Please help me to learn the art of gentleness so that I can guide my children with the wisdom of the Holy Spirit.

Releasing Grief
& Receiving New Life

I found a poetic story in one of my journals months after I had written it. It reminds me of how important it is to catalog my thoughts each day because I never know what I really write until I come back to it in the future. What an authentic picture of forgiveness and creativity; I did not even know its beauty was hanging around in my back pocket to share. Sometimes we fill up with strength and inspiration that later give us courage and the patience to walk through the process. Mothers live lives full of patience and forgiveness. It can make us bitter, or it can make us come alive.

It's our choice. Our children are such gifts.

There's nothing like soaking in meditation and the sounds of God worship, only then to be released into a garment of child whines, demands, and tears.

What we soak in some moments gives us strength for the next wave.

We ebb and flow.

Breathe in Peace so we can exhale Life.

And when the chatter of surroundings competes with the peace of my new heart—

We make orange Jell-O.

When the boiling water bubbles and steams—and I have to tell the kids, "Step back. Do not get burned"—

I breathe. I exhale dust.

And when they are pushing and shoving to see the gelatin melt just as I pour in the cup of cold water, I breathe.

And when they nag about when it is going to be done, I grapple with my words and say:

"It will be ready when it is dark outside."

Because in reality, we are ripe when it is dark. When the sun stops shining in our direction and when the torrent blows us through the stormiest of the storms inside, we are ripe.

For forgiveness.

For the empty tomb to reveal our depravity.

For the death that comes before the emerging life.

We make orange Jell-O.

In biological and art history, the color orange symbolizes creativity and intimacy and the portion of the body that releases life (reproductive organs). Beautiful, isn't it? I did not pick orange Jell-O on purpose; it was what was in the cupboard. Sometimes when we are in life's trenches, we have to work with what we already have. Creativity and intimacy are free and forever healing. They cannot be bought in the store, but they can be found in God and within us.

This is often the case when we step into motherhood. We cannot buy all the right answers in the store, but we can look within our journey and find the answers we need. When transforming from a person without children to a mother, we find all sorts of emotions that we want to release. There are extremes everywhere—from the high of ecstatic joy to the grief of lost identity. There is life, and there is death. There was free time, and now there is none. There was quiet, and now there is crying. There was one child, and now there are sibling squabbles. It is a continual state of grieving an old season and moving into a new one. And yet, as we die to the old way of life, we understand His sacrifice. And when we submit to self-control, to pruning, and to feeling on fire sometimes, we become refined and beautified in the process. When we make orange Jell-O, we get to enjoy the treat.

It is a voyage. We lose ourselves in self-sacrifice and tame our tongue when we sometimes want to scream. It is a journey: responding to the heights of joy and the simplicities of colored gelatin. We grieve an old way of freedom, and we birth a new way of living. And in the middle, we start to understand who God is.

Day 11

If anyone is in Christ, that person is part of the new creation.
The old things have gone away, and look,
new things have arrived!

2 Corinthians 5:17 CEB

Motherhood is a combination of grieving what once was and accepting what now is. We step out of one way of living and doing, and we start walking into a whole new direction. And all of this can occur in the matter of a single day. Everything changes when a child is born, and often the mother tries to transition into her new role with a lack of sleep, a new understanding of how the world works, and much grief with which to reconcile. *Grief* is a general term used simply to express the idea of letting the old pass away; it is a perfectly normal emotion and experience during transitions. What often happens in the swirl of new life is that the mother forgets she has an opportunity to both honor and grieve the old way of doing things. I know I surely did. I was used to quiet in my mornings, an ordered routine to start my day, time to shower and wash my clothes, time to do my hair and talk with my husband or friends. What I didn't realize was that my life would now revolve around someone else, and not around me. Motherhood allows us to embrace ourselves differently when routines somewhat disappear, babies cry at any hour of the day or night, and the small act of showering seems like a gift from Heaven's gates.

When we are honest with ourselves and can honor the process of passing from the old to the new, we can experience more abundance in the present and in the future. As a mom struggles with the guilt of missing her old life, it actually is not anything to feel bad about. Instead, it is an opportunity to be aware that the transitional feelings from an old lifestyle to a new lifestyle are healthy. Motherhood is a whole new ride.

What are some activities, routines, or simple joys that you used to do before having children? How many of those activities can you still incorporate somehow, even just a little bit, into your life now? What are a few routines or activities you may need to place on hold? While you're in a season of transition, just remember that many of those activities will come back around, in a fresh form, at a later time.

A Simple Prayer

Jesus, help me to allow the process of grief to flow from me.
Give me the grace to let the old way of life go
gracefully so that I am free to be present in my new life.

Day 12

Out of his fullness we have all received grace
in place of grace already given.

John 1:16 NIV

Motherhood is hard work. Although there are books about it, there is not a manual for each of your particular children. You have been chosen to be their mother, and you are the best woman for the job.

Whether simply dealing with emotions that arise when you think of the way life used to be or working through the emotions of what is often called "mom guilt," a mom will often come face to face with the inner emotional experience of taking on the role of motherhood. Sometimes it is easy to get caught up in the concept that we have to be happy with our role as a mom all the time, that if we struggle or are unsure or have made mistakes we have done something majorly wrong. Mom guilt often invades our consciences when we simply just need a break or need an opportunity to be a person again without a role.

At my early stages of motherhood, and even at times now, I still have to remind myself to let go. Mothers can be their own worst critics, categorizing all their minute faults into a cesspool of made-up discouragement. It's important to remind yourself of God's rich mercy. He is leading the way, and His truth can come into any situation when we pray. Being a mother can sometimes feel like a job with no break, and at many times it is. On the days when you notice there is not much gas in the tank and are tempted to feel badly about your parenting skills (or when you try to fix every single mistake you may or may not have made), give yourself a bit of grace. This is the perfect time not to overanalyze but to relax and enjoy. It is the perfect time to honor yourself and your humanity, all the hard work you have done, and move forward with new self-confidence in Christ's provision for you. You are valuable and cared for.

What are some areas of mom guilt with which you repeatedly struggle? What are some mistakes you have made to which you would like to bring gentle correction? What are some mistakes that you just need to let go of? (Perfection is demeaning.) What are some ways in which you are a great mom?

Breathe in self-confidence. This is beautiful, meaningful work!

A Simple Prayer

Jesus, help me to release the mom guilt. Help me to give myself grace, to receive new life from You, and to let go of hindrances that bring anxiety instead of peace.

Day 13

Cry out in sorrow, mourn, and weep! Let your laughter become mourning and your joy become sadness.

James 4:9 CEB

Grief can come in many forms during motherhood, often in cases of miscarriage, infertility, loss of a child, or the quiet of an empty nest. Sometimes we go through these transitions personally, and other times we help carry the burden of a friend who goes through difficulties. When motherhood reflects such a great loss, it can be extremely fragile, hard to understand, and confusing. To celebrate new life and then to grieve in the aftermath creates a whirlwind of emotions that need honest attending to. There is no magical formula to make deep loss disappear, but steps can be taken to create sacred space to honor the loss and navigate through it. It's common to ask why and to have many questions related to loss, sometimes questions that don't seem to be answered on this side of Heaven. Yet, in this season of reflection and healing, there is time to honor areas in our lives or other mothers' lives that may have been stunted before they had a chance to bloom. It's a time of gentleness, to allow the feelings to flow and to await the gift of healing, because even in loss, God can show us His greatness.

What are some simple ways to honor deep loss during motherhood? What are some avenues for releasing pain in a healthy way? If you have experienced loss personally, how can you exhibit self-care in a way that nourishes your soul? If you are walking with a friend who is experiencing loss in motherhood, what are some simple acts of kindness that would help lighten the burden she is experiencing? A good friend can help heal grief with the simplicity of presence and awareness.

A Simple Prayer

Jesus, with each loss of life, may You fill us up.

Help us to be honest in our grief

and be available to Your healing.

Day 14

Know this: the LORD takes personal care of the faithful.
The LORD will hear me when I cry out to him.

Psalm 4:3 CEB

In many ways, we transition emotionally over how our schedules, time, and way of life completely change as we welcome a new child. In addition to this, we also process the way our bodies, faces, and general appearances change as we have stretched and grown and released a person into this world. Pregnancy takes its toll on our body, stress often manifests itself in a few more wrinkles than we would like, and we may carry more weight or a muffin top that we did not have before. It is this beautiful process that also causes us to look at ourselves and wonder, *What happened to me?* There is a balance between saying goodbye to a physique we once had and also stewarding the new one we now have. Movement is created in our lives by letting go of old ideals while giving acceptance to the way we look presently; moving into self-care preserves the health and body we have been given. Walking out of the old body and into the new one takes peace, hope, and motion. The best way to care for ourselves is gentleness and forward momentum. So as we say goodbye to an old body and hello to a few stretch marks, we accept the price we paid for carrying life. And then we move forward to steward this new body and holy appearance. We honor what we have been given. And if it is a bit of work, the challenge is always healthy. I always enjoy having a giant to face; it brings out the mama bear in me.

What are a few simple ways you can heal after childbirth? A little face cream and a walk can go a long way. How can you bring back some self-confidence after your body has transformed and is still coming back to a healed and whole state? Choosing a good diet is key to healing well. Healthy food and vitamins bring healing and helpful transformation. How can you add a few more fruits and vegetables to your regimen?

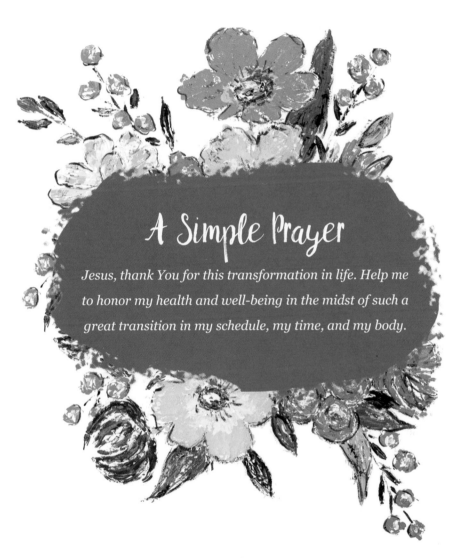

A Simple Prayer

Jesus, thank You for this transformation in life. Help me to honor my health and well-being in the midst of such a great transition in my schedule, my time, and my body.

Day 15

Therefore my heart is glad, and my glory rejoices;
My flesh also will rest in hope.

Psalm 16:9 NKJV

Acceptance is the key to happiness. When grief is released in us and when new life comes our way, we learn how to process. We say goodbye to what once was, and we say hello to what we now get to receive. It is such a gift! In the midst of it, we accept this transition. We honor, we grow, and we come to terms with our current stature with gentleness. It is in this place of self-acceptance that we can see God move in our midst.

I remember distinctly the mornings I would wake early, sit on my couch with a hot cup of coffee, and simply let tears fall from my eyes. All was quiet, and I could allow myself the space to breathe and sip. Those tender moments changed the course of my motherhood. God is faithful with our tears! And when we acknowledge what He is doing, we can face each day with a grateful and peaceful heart. We can live our day with joy and compassion. We can nurture our children with the same love we have been nurtured with by our Heavenly Father. In the transition, we start to see parts of ourselves that we did not know before. I found so many new hobbies and gifts that I never would have started without the process. I most likely would not be an author, would not love to walk and jog, and probably would never have actually started to cook anything worth eating. God bless it!

We start to experience love in a way that moves toward unconditional measures, and we start to live the way we were created to. Motherhood is a wonderful process full of highs and lows, and we get to experience it all! We have created new life, and now we continue to move forward with courage, vulnerability, and truth. We get to receive the newness of life in many forms.

How can you celebrate today? How can you celebrate where you are and what you have become? Look back on God's faithfulness and practice gratitude. Accept yourself for the brave woman that you are; be open to the surprises God has in store for you!

A Simple Prayer

Jesus, please show me what true acceptance looks like in my life. Help me live a life in faith and vulnerability and with great care and excitement for the future.

The Comparison Game

One of the best ways to thwart unworthiness or comparison is to look for the good.

If we struggle with feeling unworthy or comparing ourselves to other moms, it does not mean that we are a mess. It means that we need a personal upgrade. It means that at some point, we lost the joy of who we are and we need to reconnect with ourselves. Though social media often can make us feel worse about ourselves as moms, it is important to remember that change starts with us! Happiness is in front of us, not on a screen or in a perfectly controlled world.

Several years ago, I started on a proactive journey to find out who God made me to be, both as a person and as a mom. God provided clues in advance for me to see that I would face many challenges. In reality, it was really kind of Him to be so reaffirming when I faced a desert. *He is always handing me treasure maps!*

It is not as if identity is a new topic in our society. It can feel as if everyone is trying to find herself these days. I have had the opportunity to "be myself" many times in my life—but with this season of life called *motherhood*, it felt more definitive. I experienced an actual and physical shift in my body that made this identity come into a much clearer picture. This shift has four names: Ella, Micah (who is now with Jesus), Lucy, and Oliver.

Becoming a mother is a new season of identity. It brings forth parts of us that are beautiful and nurturing and natural, and it also opens up broken parts in need of beauty, nurturing, and love.

When God hands us a miracle, sometimes it feels like we have to learn how to help it live and grow and survive and thrive. And this can turn into a confidence builder and a self-esteem crusher all at the same time. It can feel like our identity, confidence, and personhood are in a state of crisis.

Typically, when our self-esteem has taken a beating with bad toddler behavior or sleepless nights or other unplanned circumstances, it is easy to want to look at ourselves in a dim light and then compare ourselves to the mom next door who always seems to have it together.

Here is the funny part, though: no mother has it all together. We are all trying to figure this thing out. What mothers need are gentle, loving, truthful, and graceful supporters. There is no time for comparison; it doesn't work. No two mothers are the same, and no two children are the same. Just as I need grace as a mother, you need grace as a mother, and she needs need grace as a mother too.

So when our insecurity or our judgments or our pain want to brashly rear their heads, instead let's extend a hand to one another. Let's open the vulnerable door to our hearts to let the light in. Let's remember who God made us to be as individual mothers, sisters, and confidants. Let's remind ourselves and each other that we are exactly what our children need, and they are exactly what we need. Because that is the beauty of how God works; He is always providing for us.

Day 16

Let us not grow weary while doing good, for in due season
we shall reap if we do not lose heart.

Galatians 6:9 NKJV

One of the quickest ways to lose your joy in motherhood is unbelief in your worth and mothering abilities. God made you perfectly able and fit for your child's innate needs. What often hinders us from mothering well is unreconciled grief and harboring mistakes and anxiety. Yet even in our areas of weakness, as we submit those to God, they become our biggest assets as parents. Sometimes it is easy to look at other mothers and compare everything from the organic dish soap down to the type of binkie (if you even use a binkie). One thing is for sure: moms need time to be reminded of the divine way in which we became mothers. It was God's hand in our lives. The love of two particular people made a baby who is completely unique and attuned to respond to the gifts and parenting of those two people. It is beautiful, miraculous, and cannot be compared to another family's experience. We can gain wisdom and understanding from other families; we can exchange tips and advice. But when we step onto the slippery slope of thinking that we are not enough or that we are not doing it right or that we have failed, we know it is time to step back and realign ourselves. It is a great idea to find support in a few close friends during this time—people who can support you in your unique parenting style and who can remind you that you are doing a great job, especially with the hardest and most meaningful job there is!

What are areas in your mothering where you often fall into the comparison trap? What are skills you would like to grow? What are weaknesses you would like to strengthen? Who are your closest family members or friends at this time?

A Simple Prayer

Jesus, please give me the grace to be honest about my successes and my failures as a mother. Give me opportunities to share my strengths, and give me support to nurture areas that need growth.

Day 17

Therefore let us not judge one another anymore, but rather resolve this, not to put a stumbling block or a cause to fall in our brother's way.

Romans 14:13 NKJV

Comparison robs us of joy, contentment, and confidence. Constantly looking at other mothers and the way they parent can turn into our quickest downfall. If you are having a difficult time looking around without judging yourself, the best thing to do is take a self-inventory. Taking a break from social media or friendships where conversation is not fruitful is a great first step. If you are consistently finding yourself struggling in a certain area, you can find another mother who has walked your path. Often, we can find support and strength in friendships with women who have struggled in similar areas of identity and mothering. When they have overcome hardships, their advice can give you some tools for your journey.

When struggling with comparison in any form, it is best to set boundaries with what triggers you and find support with those who can build into you. It is the best of both worlds, and you can gain forward momentum both with your weaknesses and with your strengths. Looking around for the approval of others simply means you're actually searching for something you need. Sometimes an older friend is the perfect support for this season! Whether that is your mom, grandmother, or an older family member, a friend from church, or a counselor, you deserve to find rest and support for this season of life! Mothering brings up a variety of insecurities, and it is perfectly good to bring in some boundaries and also some unconditional love and truth.

Do you have several people in your support system whom you can call for encouragement and prayer? Perhaps ask an older family member or wise friend to commit to praying for you weekly. Knowing someone is in your corner can help ease the transition for new parents and even seasoned ones. It also helps new moms to be encouraged in their personal journeys without allowing themselves to feel defeated by the appearance of others.

Who can help support you in your journey? Look for an accountability friendship, someone who will challenge you to be you and also give you the support needed to make that a reality.

A Simple Prayer

Jesus, thank You for giving me the life I have.
Would You give me access to the support I need
for growth, maturity, and joy as a mother?

Day 18

Wherever there is jealousy and selfish ambition,
there is disorder and everything that is evil.

James 3:16 CEB

The first step for practicing self-awareness is opening our eyes and ears to the lies we believe about ourselves. When we recognize what our triggers are (for example, jealousy, comparison, negative self-talk), we have the opportunity to find a solution. Many times the negative feeling we are experiencing is actually just the opposite of who we are meant to be. If we are jealous, we really need connection to our true selves. If we compare ourselves to others, we really are just looking for validation of our identity. If we talk or think negatively about ourselves, it is an opportunity to find a friend who can remind us of our true worth. Small steps lead to big changes.

I remember looking at people's clean houses when I was a young mom, and all I could think about was how much I missed having a clean house and order in my life! The reality of the situation was that I needed to give myself at least one area in my home that was clean and organized at all times. This simple act gave me peace and reminded me that I would have routine again someday. It also allowed me to stop feeling frustrated when other parts of my home became a mess with food, baby toys, laundry, and spilled milk.

When trying to connect with your true self, fuel your energy toward what is good. If you are a working mom who would like to stay at home, look into a few ways that you can make money from home. If you are a stay-at-home mom and need to work outside the home, look for a way to do that but still maintain your time with your children. If you wish your child would behave better, look inside yourself at what behavior you can change. Kids mimic their parents. If you wish your child would listen to you, listen to them. If you wish you had more mother friends, go to the park and be a friend. If you wish your mom body was back to prepregnancy weight, take your kids for a walk. If you want a clean house, maybe just start with one clean room. You will thank yourself in a million ways. Comparison breeds bitterness, and movement breeds joy.

What is a small step forward that you can make today for growth? What is a limiting belief with which you struggle? Remind yourself that small steps are the beginning of freedom!

A Simple Prayer

Jesus, give me the grace and the bravery to be self-aware.
Help me see the joy in my identity so that I can be whole
and be a better steward of my environment.

Day 19

I'm also asking you, loyal friend, to help these women
who have struggled together with me in the ministry of the gospel,
along with Clement and the rest of my coworkers
whose names are in the scroll of life.

Philippians 4:3 CEB

One of the best ways to build a good support system is to leave behind unhealthy relationships. Motherhood is a vulnerable and emotional time, and it is important to be particular about whom you let into your life during this season. If someone is repeatedly setting you up for failure with his or her words or company, the first step is to take constructive criticism into account, and the second step is to make a healthy boundary for yourself. It does not mean all relationships have to go to the curb, but it does mean that reevaluating your support system at this time may be important. Self-esteem and joy are vital to mothering well. If you are supported well, you can be the best mother you want to be. If the support you have been leaning on is not grounded in goodness, it is an appropriate time to look at other avenues for nurturing your soul. A happy mother is a confident mother, and you deserve to be the best!

Think about some areas in your life that could be hindering your innate support system. It could be people, unhealthy food, time wasted in unfruitful ways, or many other things. Remind yourself that you deserve the best. Remember to allow for constructive criticism, but also surround yourself with support and people who are trying to build you up. You have every right to be particular! Your motherhood depends on it.

A Simple Prayer

Jesus, thank You for being my ultimate support system.

Please give me wisdom in choosing the friends and

relationships that I bring close to me during this season.

Help me to receive constructive criticism;

help me to understand my innate worth.

Day 20

God also vouched for their message with signs, amazing things, various miracles, and gifts from the Holy Spirit, which were handed out the way he wanted.

Hebrews 2:4 CEB

Nurturing confidence and identity (outside of mothering) is a great tool for self-growth and gaining new skills. One of the best ways to be a great mother is actually to forget you are a mother every once in a while! Sharpening personal skills and talents outside of mothering brings you back to a clearer version of yourself and a clearer version of your kids. It can be just the boost you need in order to enjoy your children in a fresh way.

Mothering is new and challenging. Remembering old gifts and expressions you had before becoming a mother helps you stay balanced and keeps you out of your own head. Identity is key to great mothering and stops the struggle of comparison. A mom who is happy with herself and the growing version of herself is happy when nurturing the growing versions of those around her, even in the midst of temper tantrums, dirty diapers, and sleepless nights. I am a better mother when I am expressing myself as a person in addition to being a mother. For me, moving my body, writing, or engaging in art is a great way to remember myself as Sarah instead of just "Mom".

Be kind to yourself! Remember the joys of your own childhood and identity. Do not let the responsibilities of your new life steal the joy you had when all you had to manage was yourself. Don't compare yourself to others when you can connect with yourself in a deeper way. Go on a creative date all by yourself. Choose a day on the calendar, mark it down, and go do something you used to do all the time. Remember the ease of freedom and a carefree existence! It will fuel you to love and give more abundantly.

A Simple Prayer

Jesus, thank You for who You have created me to be
before becoming a mother. Help me to remember
who I was when responsibility was not at the forefront;
help me to remember how to play.

Self-Acceptance & Peace

I love that word. *Acceptance.*

Acceptance has been my golden ticket to peace. Kind of like my youngest, Oliver.

I knew while I was pregnant with my middle, Lucy, that there would also be one more child. And when God surprised us with a plus sign on a pregnancy test, I was somewhat not surprised—because I knew I needed him. His little life would help me find this peace and acceptance I had been looking for.

There is something about having a third child and going to zone-defense as a daily routine that teaches me peace. Moms of three-plus kids are always outnumbered. The house will not be perfect. My energy will be spread more thinly across the board. I do not have enough hands for each child. If more than one person is talking, I cannot possibly answer them all. It is sometimes chaos. But it is beautiful chaos.

The days I find myself most stressed out about my house being totally out of control are the days I am not willing to accept that I am living in a season when my house is just going to be somewhat out of control. It does not mean that I am lazy and do not take steps to clean out the oven after I have neglected it for the last five years. Wait, what? No, it just means that I focus on the task at hand, and I have to learn to *let the rest of it go* for now. As a young mom, acceptance comes in the simple fact that life is a bit overwhelming in this season. And no matter how much we might want to keep the floor clean, it's probably not going to happen. And for now, that is OK!

I have been the queen of nervous exhaustion; I previously was an energizer bunny who would never stop, but I didn't realize for the longest time that fumes are not actually gas. Add to that three kids who are three years old and under, and you get a hot mess. A *hot mess*, I tell ya. Sometimes I have to rethink things and wonder how I got there. The worst part about that season was that I simply couldn't accept that I just had to let go.

But that is now my ticket: learning to accept the season I am in. And my youngest's tender temperament has been the perfect reminder to relish the moment, whether the floor is mopped or not. Because if we never get to the acceptance part, we will always be trying to fix something. And if I am always trying to fix something, I am not really enjoying anything. I have been given a life and a motherhood to delight in with three of the cutest little people on the planet.

It is amazing and simple, really: accept that life is somewhat chaotic instead of constantly trying to paddle upstream. We often choose to paddle upstream; that's the crazy part. When we do, we usually have a white-knuckle grip and end up nowhere. At least I do.

But when we loosen up, we can embrace each moment. It is so much more wonderful to show up to our own lives—our messy, chaotic, finding-peace-in-the-crazy lives. Because when we do, we actually start to dream and build and bloom right in the midst of the dirt and soil and sunshine.

And, in turn, that's where I often write poetry about those very experiences:

Acceptance in the Tares

So let the wheat grow with the tares

That His glory would be manifest in me

This has never been about my performance

But about His Goodness

So I offer up my Death of self

Not because I am unworthy, or not enough,

or nothing—that is religion

But because when I see the emptiness of manmade effort,

I absorb the worth of God-made Design

He never made me nothing

He always made me something

And as the wheat grows with the tares

I see His beauty over me, in me, through me

So let the wheat grow with the tares . . .

Day 21

I will praise You, for I am fearfully and wonderfully made; Marvelous are Your works, And that my soul knows very well.

Psalm 139:14 NKJV

i t is said that a person needs to hear something new almost thirty times before he or she actually starts to believe it, and that a person usually needs a topic repeated in a variety of ways in order to make it settle in. We are on Day 21 of our journey to a joyful motherhood, and if you are not clear what we need most as mothers, here it is again in a couple key words: *self-care* and *acceptance*! The best mothers are those who are well loved and well nurtured as women. We already have perfect and complete acceptance from a loving God; Jesus has made this path straight for us. The next and very crucial step is for us to love ourselves and care for ourselves. God can love us and care for us, but if we do not love and care for ourselves, we set ourselves up for loss. Of course, support from a loving spouse, our children, and our friends brings fullness to our lives! But we as women often need to encourage ourselves to come into a more abundant stance of self-acceptance and self-love. Moms are perpetually hard on themselves, categorizing the faults and failures and fears of every day. Spending intentional time caring for yourself (even if it's simply forty days of reading this book) is a great place to start.

List five things about yourself that you absolutely love. List five ways you love your family as well. You are doing a great job!

A Simple Prayer

Jesus, let me see the good in myself. Help me to celebrate who I am in all the messiness and chaos and beauty that is called new life.

Day 22

But I will remember the Lord's deeds; yes, I will remember your
wondrous acts from times long past.

Psalm 77:11 CEB

The problem of self-acceptance often can be traced to challenges from our childhood. What we sometimes see in ourselves as weak parenting skills are actually patterns that have been passed on to us from the way we were raised. As we see the weak spots, it is important to nurture the lacking areas. When wounds are triggered, it is the perfect opportunity for God to bring healing. After the healing comes, so does the new mindset. We always have the opportunity to accept God's gift in our lives and then choose a new behavior; He loves to shower His mercy and grace on us! If we are constantly anxious and react toward our children with haste and a loud voice, we need peace in our lives. We need our own trauma healed. Mothering can be overwhelming, but so can peace, healing, and joy.

We can do this by giving our wounds to God, allowing Him to fill us with His peace, and then choosing a better position of care. There can be different patterns passed down to us that we would like to interrupt and re-create differently for our children. As we accept where we have been and what we need, we can break cycles that do not foster a healthy environment for our family. If you feel you can't do this alone, please reach out for help from your church or a counselor. You are not weak for reaching out; you are strong!

What are some patterns in your life or in your parenting that you would like to interrupt? Do you remember where these patterns started? Can you go back to areas in your childhood that might be in need of restoration, of being given over to God for new provision?

A Simple Prayer

Jesus, thank You for the foundation I was given in childhood.

Help me to acknowledge patterns that need to be interrupted

and re-created with honesty, humility, and forgiveness.

Day 23

They will burst into bloom, and rejoice with joy and singing. They will receive the glory of Lebanon, the splendor of Carmel and Sharon. They will see the Lord's glory, the splendor of our God.

Isaiah 35:2 CEB

Bloom where you are planted; it is the best way to start loving and accepting yourself. When we learn how to build where we are, we take baby steps toward significance. We can make small choices daily that can help propel us into a life and motherhood full of joy, peace, and fulfillment. Once we start becoming seasoned in our own healing work, we start to live with much more fervor and gratitude. It is often these small daily choices we make that bring us to a place of inner peace and contentment. In the slow and steady of life, we make progress. If self-acceptance were a skin care regimen, we would see great results with daily use over a period of time. And who doesn't love that? A facial is wonderful every once in a while to go deeper and to enhance what we are already doing, but the overall most sustainable changes come from our daily disciplines. This is how we bloom where we are. We start with the simple act of caring for ourselves.

What can you do now for self-acceptance? Do you need to be heard? Write in a journal or tell a story. Do you need understanding? Find a friend who is a great listener. Do you need support? Ask for help. It almost seems obvious, but self-acceptance often lies in small tasks. From the small choice to step toward your true nature, you start to shift the stress and self-rejection out of your heart. It has worked for me! When I take a small step, I always feel more like my real self.

How can you bloom where you are planted? What is a small but steady goal in one area of your life that you would like to pursue? Diet, exercise, faith, skin care, parenting skills, a hobby (for example, writing, dancing, cooking)? Give yourself permission to start in baby steps toward a dream or goal that has always been in your heart.

A Simple Prayer

Jesus, give me the vision to start with small steps of self-acceptance in the here and now. Help me to be diligent in my daily disciplines so that I can become the best version of myself.

Day 24

You've given me the shield of your salvation; your strong hand has supported me; your help has made me great.

Psalm 18:35 CEB

Once you start growing in your own self-confidence and gifts, find a group where you can get connected and share. Whether it is a small group of friends, a church, a class, or a club, finding a place to invest is key to growing and blooming well. With the support and encouragement of other people, you will see the fruit of your life grow exponentially. Surround yourself with people who want to see you do well as a person and as a parent; they may even end up asking to hold your baby or babysit for you! Surround yourself with people who have resources and wisdom to share with you and who you can also support with your own wisdom and resources. As the exchange grows between your self-acceptance, personal growth, and the opportunities presented by a support system, you will see your spirit being filled up in new and exciting ways. You will also see this happen for your children because they love a mom who is happy. As you bloom, so will they.

After you have found a place to plug in, ask God how He might want you to participate. Sometimes we just need friendship and rest without much activity (because moms are always active); other times we are ready to serve in a more formal context through a part-time job or as a leader within an organization (for example, a coach, or teacher, and so on). Be aware of what is best for your particular situation. You know your limits, and you also know your goals. Choose what is right for you, and start to build into your new future!

A Simple Prayer

Thank You, Jesus, for my gifts and desires.

Help me to plug into the right community,

with the right time requirements, and where my goals

and dreams are supported.

Day 25

Strength and honor are her clothing; she is confident about the future.

Proverbs 31:25 CEB

Dare to dream! When basic needs are met and our self-concept is healthy and alive, there is plenty of room to play. This is where, as mothers, we give ourselves the opportunity to explore and create. We give ourselves room to hope and pray and dream again, continually bringing us into a place of discovery, growth, newfound freedom, self-care, and generosity for others. Every mother has her own unique desires for her family and calling. Some moms want to homeschool, to bring their kids in closely, and to dream as a unit in this way. Other moms may send their children to school while they continue to prepare their homes or take care of other children. Other mothers may want to reenter the workforce and have their family get involved in community-centered service projects. Still other families may get really connected within a church body. There are so many options, and no one way is designated as the right way. There are many right ways! It is at this place that you can choose how you would like to give. Whether it is continuing to build into your own family first (perhaps having more children or cultivating a healthy and close environment) or extending out to the community in some way, this is the place where dreams become reality. When the mom is healthy and happy, the whole family comes into alignment and into new opportunities to dream and succeed.

What are some of the dreams you have for your family, both short and long term? I always want my family to eat at the dinner table each weekend (short term), and I also want my family to participate in community projects together (possibly long term). Work on a short family mission statement that covers your family's values and goals. Who are you as a family, and where are you going? Have fun!

A Simple Prayer

Jesus, I want to dream! Align my heart and desires to Your

will so I can dream, explore, and serve my family.

The Cycles of Giving & Self-Care

When David and I bought our first house, we thought it needed something. You know, something that would bring flair and fun and comfort.

So we bought ourselves a Saint Bernard.

Oh, Howie. How I adored him. I couldn't imagine life without him. How the kids loved him! The minute they arrived home after being born, they were welcomed with a big, slobbery kiss.

He was big and fluffy (sadly, he is now in doggie heaven) the best pillow around. Every morning, as I would rest my head on his belly, he would rest his giant of a head across my face, and though I could barely breathe, I loved it.

And then I would walk downstairs to start my day. I would see dog food all over the kitchen floor, mixed with crumbs cast down from the high chair. I would sit down on the couch with my cup of hot coffee only to realize I had rested my arm in a two-inch-long streak of slobbery goo. And let's not talk about how many times my vacuum cleaner broke from overuse picking up dog fur.

But there was something about that gentle giant that wooed us. Just like love.

Sometimes love is messy, like muddy paws all over the couch. Sometimes it is heavy, like a Saint Bernard who thinks he is a lap dog. Sometimes it is protective, like watching through the window while Ella took her naps. And sometimes it is astonishing, like finding a monster of a dog in our bed eating a bone from the butcher. Yes, he leaves a big slobbery mess in my bed, which creates more laundry. But, I wouldn't change a thing about him.

When it comes down to it, Howie made me a better person. Just like my children do. Just like love does. He was messy and loveable and tested every bit of my patience.

Love is patient, love is kind, it isn't jealous, it doesn't brag, it isn't arrogant, it isn't rude, it doesn't seek its own advantage, it isn't irritable, it doesn't keep a record of complaints, it isn't happy with injustice, but it is happy with the truth. Love puts up with all things, trusts in all things, hopes for all things, endures all things. Love never fails.

1 Corinthians 13:4–8a CEB

Howie comforted parts of our family that were broken and in need of a hug. Dogs have amazing healing power; they are amazing complements to children. He cuddled at just the right time. He sat at attention waiting for his treat like the sweetest of army soldiers. He made me laugh as he scavenged under each child's high chair, eagerly awaiting a dropped blueberry or piece of toast.

And the games he would play! He scratched at the door for an hour to come inside, and every time I got to the door to open it, he ran away (and smiled). The kids would laugh. He liked to play, and honestly, sometimes it tested us all. It highlighted the parts in me that still needed a little lovin' or carefree energy, just like the muddy paws and the slobber on the walls and the chunk of our budget labeled "lint rollers."

But it is a beautiful paradox, isn't it? Kind of like marriage. Kind of like parenting. A lot like love.

If dogs are a person's best friend, then every mom should have one. There is something in the love of a dog that covers and nourishes us in the messiness, in the exercise, and in the picking up huge bags of dog food at the grocery store. So much of having a Saint Bernard taught me about the healing power of generosity and of sharing love. And just as much, it taught me about how to care for and nurture myself and let myself just be. It taught the kids protection, care, and comfort. And more importantly, Howie teaches unconditional love.

Dogs and kids belong together. They both teach us how to love and how to give. They also teach us where the end of our rope is so that we can learn how to take care of ourselves and heal. We learn how to place limits on our giving as we also learn how to receive cuddles and nourishment unconditionally.

Giving is what mothers do. It just is. And if the love of a mother could be bottled into a pet, it would be as big and jovial and gentle as a Saint Bernard.

Day 26

But this I say: He who sows sparingly will also reap sparingly,
and he who sows bountifully will also reap bountifully.
So let each one give as he purposes in his heart,
not grudgingly or of necessity; for God loves a cheerful giver.

2 Corinthians 9:6–7 NKJV

The default mode of a mother is giver. Giver of life, giver of time, giver of nurture. If there is any type of serving required, a mother learns how to do it. As moms, we give all day long, often to those who cannot help themselves, especially with children in the early years. Caretaking is a genuine gift but can also be taxing without the proper boundaries. Self-care is the key to giving well and with purity. Managing these boundaries, self-care, and generosity looks like a dance; it takes practice, rhythm, and learning how to flow to the music. As we are cared for by the Greatest Giver of all, we learn how to start releasing that same care into the people around us.

The first step is always to listen. Take a few minutes of quiet time to ask God what it is that you need from Him today. How can you understand God's nature as a Giver today? When we see our lack, we can receive His fullness. Becoming self-aware with our basic needs can bring proper alignment for our souls; this helps us then fill in the basic needs of our families.

A Simple Prayer

Jesus, thank You for being the Greatest Giver of life.
Give me the grace to walk in your flow of generosity,
tending to my own self-care and then overflowing
to others around me.

Day 21

Finally, brethren, whatever things are true, whatever things
are noble, whatever things are just, whatever things
are pure, whatever things are lovely, whatever things are of good
report, if there is any virtue and if there is anything
praiseworthy—meditate on these things.

Philippians 4:8 NKJV

It is important for you to know, as a person and as a mother, what fills you up. How do you fuel your love tank? Some call these the Love Languages (how we give and receive love), and they are definitely that. Do you like quality time? Quiet time? A hug? A walk? Being served? Serving? The list can go on and on. The key to filling up your life with thanksgiving is to find the ways by which you can replace the love and life you give away on a regular basis. As we communicate to others around us the ways in which we receive love, we can also learn the best ways in which they give and receive love. And when we are in the stream, stemming from the perfect love of God, we are able to ebb and flow with the nature of generosity. Our family becomes like a river, no one lacking but always moving forward and producing life where it is needed.

Spend some time honing in on your favorite ways to be loved. Share those with your family. Think of ways that you can incorporate this kind of love into your life daily so that you always feel like you have been refreshed in a way that helps you serve better.

A Simple Prayer

Jesus, help me to remember myself in the giving.

Remind me of the ways I feel most nurtured.

Help me to remember to nourish myself daily as a devotion

and honor to You and to myself.

Day 28

Love suffers long and is kind; love does not envy; love does not parade itself, is not puffed up; does not behave rudely, does not seek its own, is not provoked, thinks no evil; does not rejoice in iniquity, but rejoices in the truth; bears all things, believes all things, hopes all things, endures all things.

1 Corinthians 13:4–7 NKJV

After we learn how we like to receive love, it is equally important to figure out our favorite way to give love. Sometimes they are the same, and sometimes they are different. When we can highlight the ways in which we like to give, it opens us to more outlets through which to fill up our love tanks as mothers. Motherhood is almost one constant motion, and it is important to know where we can get small charges of energy here and there. Finding ways to serve that provide us with joy keeps us fresh and alive; it serves our own hearts and souls while we also give love away. Soon enough, these favorite ways of receiving love and sharing love can give us the capacity to give out in ways that may not be as natural for us but that might be most important to those around us.

Think about your favorite ways to give love. What are a few tangible tasks that you love performing for your family? In the giving, we can always receive as well; sometimes we just need to find the right outlet.

A Simple Prayer

Jesus, help me to recognize my favorite ways

to give love. Show me opportunities

to love well in ways that I enjoy.

Day 29

I give you a new commandment: Love each other.
Just as I have loved you, so you also must love each other.

John 13:34 CEB

After we take responsibility for ourselves and the ways in which we enjoy receiving and giving love, we have a great capacity within us to nurture the ways our loved ones also give and receive love. Sometimes the ways our families accept love is contrary to our inherent nature, but since we have learned how to cultivate our own "love life," we now have the capacity to give from a full cup. Take time to listen and to ask your family how they best receive and give love. Because of the God-given functions of a family, we often find that where we have deficits, our family has filling. And where our family has deficits, we have filling. Sometimes what we most need is just to be aware of those needs! Set aside time today to ask your family about their favorite ways to learn, love, and grow. Write them down and keep them in a place where you can continue to review them. Make a small goal this week both to give in a way your family receives and also to give in a way you love. Watch the responses that follow.

How did you feel this week? Did you have more energy? What worked well? What might need tweaking?

A Simple Prayer

Jesus, thank You for filling up my cup!
Give me listening ears to honor the way
my family members receive love.

Day 30

May the Lord cause you to increase and enrich your love for each other and for everyone in the same way as we also love you.

1 Thessalonians 3:12 CEB

Sometimes the best way to exchange love in your family is simply connection and one-on-one dates. Quality time with those you love in a setting that is focused and without distractions makes for the best kind of exchange. If you are married, it is equally important to have time with your husband as it is with your kids because out of your marriage will flow the teamwork that your children need to thrive. One-on-one dates with your kids (especially if you have multiple children) will also give them a time for safe expression, making choices, and the intimate connection that may have started to give way to the tasks of the day and managing a household. Connection is the key to giving well. Without connection, the generosity will feel stagnant and like a chore instead of an outflow of healthy love.

Choose days on the calendar each month as date nights for yourself as well as your family. Make time in your busy schedule for your entire family but also one-on-one time. Let your children choose what they would like to do. Give them a chance to express the connection they need and would like with you. As you do this, you will find that your giving will grow, and it will be more fulfilling for your time together.

A Simple Prayer

*Jesus, help us to carve out sacred time for connection
as a family. Give us opportunities for one-on-one
depth and intimacy.*

Placing an Emphasis on Presence

There are many, many reasons why I am grateful for my kids. I can't even begin to count the ways they have enriched, transformed, and revived my life. Their simple smiles, their honest wit, their vivacious love of life—even if it just means going to the grocery store or to the bank. They restore my gratitude for all the little things, and even though I fail and stumble at times, I always learn from lessons they teach me— you know, all the stuff about myself I didn't want to look at but which I'm faced with in the form of their little eyes. Yes, those lessons. I am grateful for my children showing me the hard things, not even intentionally, but just in the way they react to life. Yet, out of all the joys and the difficult days, I think what I most appreciate about my kids is that they teach me how to be present—and that teaches me how to be loved. All kids really want is for their parents to be *with* them. Most of the time it does not even matter what we are doing, just as long as we are together. And it is in those small moments of being together that I can appreciate the idiosyncrasies of each of them. It is when I slow down that I notice that there is a dimple under Ella's right eye that shows itself when she smiles (or cries). It is when I slow down that Lucy comes over to me just to hug my neck. It is when I slow down that Oliver says, "I love you Mama" with an honesty that gives me breath.

It is in the slowdown.

There is peace. And there is presence.

It seems that in a world of doing, everything tries to steal away from this time of presence. Make sure the house is spotless. Make sure you are at this activity or that function. Make sure the clothes are washed and ironed. Make sure dinner is cooked (and always organic). Make sure they get time to exercise. Make sure *you* get time to exercise. Make sure you do not lose contact with the outside world. Make sure you are following the guidelines in this parenting how-to book. Make sure . . . Make sure . . . Make sure.

All of a sudden I am tired just from reading that paragraph.

But when I am present, I am not so tired. It does not mean that I still do not fall hard onto my pillow each night—because I surely do. It is tiring with a baby on your hip, a baby in your belly, and a three-year-old holding onto your hand. And yet, the load is lifted for all of us when we are present.

When I am not looking over what I "should" be doing for them, I am enjoying them. When I am not thinking of the to-do list that so easily stacks up, it is easy to respond favorably to, "Mama do it" and "Can we play outside?" and "Let's go to the store!"

I have a pastor friend who once shared how a newborn baby can be compared to the Presence of God. It is one of my favorite metaphors. When that baby shows up, everything is focused on it. Feed the baby, change the baby, and hold the baby when he or she is crying. We steward everything around the new life we have been given. And even though we might have multiple babies and responsibilities that have to be shared, it is still the same.

So many of the problems in our world revolve around the fact that our families are broken—that we cannot steward what we have (while packing in more activities anyway). The statistics of fatherless kids are heartbreaking. Families fight. People do not talk to one another. Children suffer.

If we lived in a world that slowed down, that was not quite so focused on being productive, that was not so ill-equipped with false responsibility, I think we might find more peace. I think if we lived with a messier house during the day, we might make room for more creativity and joy instead of just clean kitchen floors.

I find this peace in the presence of my family. They are presents to me. They teach me presence. And in presence, love is found. And so are acceptance and joy and laughter.

It is definitely a treat when a mom gets an opportunity to get to the outside world for self-care. It is a necessity. I might get a pedicure or an afternoon to myself, but I find that I can start to get bored after a few hours away. I long for the presence again.

And that is the real gift of motherhood.

Day 31

The Lord is my shepherd. I lack nothing.
He lets me rest in grassy meadows; he leads me to restful waters.

Psalm 23:1–2 CEB

What a mother most often yearns for is a heart of rest. When we are at peace, we are not in need, not in panic, and not in a state of anxiety or depression. In the quiet, we can drink Living Water. Sometimes a vacation from normal life is necessary to be refreshed and recharged, but more than that, the best type of vacation is when we can be refreshed by our daily lives. When we start to move and live by the hand of our Shepherd, we can be revived and refreshed in even the most energetic and exhausting of circumstances.

There are days when I completely unplug—well, except for my morning coffee and essential oils. Those are my necessities! But in the sense of media, extra noise, the world around me, and an overcrowded schedule, I completely turn things off. It's during those days when I can hear myself more clearly and express myself more thoughtfully that I can also enjoy God more. And when I settle into Him on purpose, my soul finds delight and care in a multitude of ways.

Let's spend this next five days memorizing Psalm 23; it is the perfect way to reconnect with and relish our Father. As we quiet ourselves, we can find everything we need within His heart.

Memorize verses 1–2 today. whether that means you write it out, speak it out loud, or simply post it on your mirror. Take the time to reflect on Psalm 23:1–2 today.

A Simple Prayer

Father, You are my Shepherd. I do not need a thing. You have given me everything. You have given me rest and peace during my trials and tribulations. You restore my soul.

Day 32

*He keeps me alive. He guides me in proper paths
for the sake of his good name.*

Psalm 23:3 CEB

Often, our best method of warfare is to memorize the Bible. Sometimes we just need to remember the Truth because His truth is life to our bones and refreshment to our hearts. As we go back to the Source, we rewire our minds and our thoughts. When all other plans fail, God does not. Just as He spoke the Word and it was, when He speaks over us, we can breathe again. And when we can take a gulp of His original breath in us, we go down the paths of righteousness. We live out lives of peace and joy and goodwill toward everyone in our path, especially toward the little ones that He has given us to steward. Isn't that rich?

In a world where something is constantly being sold in order for us to feel better, God gives us His best at any time that we need Him.

Let's continue to meditate on the goodness of God. Take a walk outside, and allow the fresh air to land on your face. Be guided by your Good Shepherd, and enjoy His company. Memorize verse 3 today.

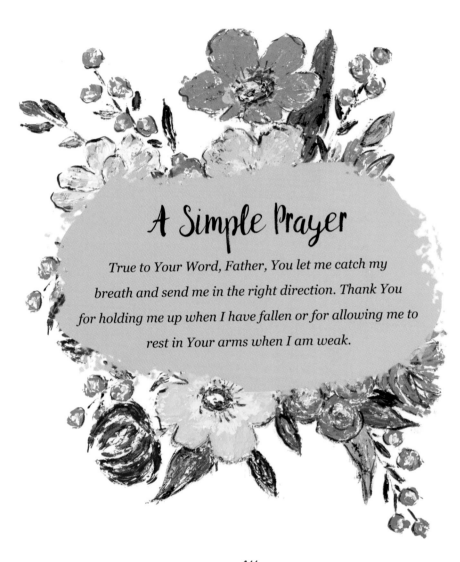

A Simple Prayer

True to Your Word, Father, You let me catch my breath and send me in the right direction. Thank You for holding me up when I have fallen or for allowing me to rest in Your arms when I am weak.

Day 33

Even when I walk through the darkest valley, I fear no danger be-cause you are with me. Your rod and your staff—they protect me.

Psalm 23:4 CEB

There will always be times of growth and trust in parenting. And even when times get difficult and struggles arise, we can remember who loves us. We remember who the biggest supporter of mothers is. When we fail, when we meet challenges that we do not feel prepared for, we can go back to the Source. *God loves us.* God loves you. He knows everything about you and has provided for every need you have.

As we give way to children by preparing, birthing, giving, grieving, and resting (and then giving even more), we always end up back at the Source. He is the Alpha and the Omega; He is the beginning and the end. Everything we need for life and godliness are found in Him. God is there in the darkest of nights and in the brightest of mornings, and He keeps us safe and secure by reminding us of His love.

Let's continue resting in His care for us by embracing His Word again today. Memorize and meditate on verse 4. Perhaps have a short time of confession and release, while relishing the fact that His covering is our protection. He never fails.

A Simple Prayer

Heavenly Father, even when my pathway goes through
Death Valley, I will not be afraid when You walk at my side.
Your trusty Shepherd's crook makes me feel secure.
I know that You are there to protect me from any evil
that tries to war against me.

Day 34

You set a table for me right in front of my enemies. You bathe my head in oil; my cup is so full it spills over!

Psalm 23:5 CEB

In our Father and in our circumstances, we have everything we need to eat. There is always enough food for us. He leads us into all the right circumstances to feed our souls. No matter what is going on around us, He always has enough resources for us. Just as we are always trying to comfort and care for our children, God delights in comforting and caring for us.

As a mother, when comparison, failures, exhaustion, and depression run their course, we need to be reminded that we have everything we need to thrive. We are the best mothers possible for our children. God gave us the DNA we have for a purpose, and it matches the DNA of our children for their purpose. As we are honest with our own emotions, we close the gaps between what we lack within our own lives. As we close those gaps, we automatically set ourselves up to help bridge and nurture any gaps in our children's lives. We become prepared as we nurture what we have been given. As our heart stays open to forgiveness, we become whole. And as we become whole, we make our children whole. It is a beautiful cycle. We forever drink of blessings.

Memorize verse 5 today, and take a bubble bath while you're at it!

A Simple Prayer

Jesus, You serve me a six-course dinner right in front of my enemies. You revive my drooping head; my cup brims with blessings. It is my prayer that any blessings that I receive I give back to those around me.

Day 35

Yes, goodness and faithful love will pursue me all the days of my life,
and I will live in the LORD's house as long as I live.

Psalm 23:6 CEB

Make a point to remember, each and every day, that motherhood is beautiful. In each diaper change and each cutting of mini-sandwiches, a mother gets to live a life of peace and joy and care. A mother gets to nurture her children. This is the beauty of God in our midst! With each death of our old selves and our old mindsets, there is great life. As mothers, we are blessed to be the ones who get to steward that gift. Our bodies actually manifest heaven coming to earth; we are the home for creating a human being. It is a privilege to do so, and it is an honor.

Being a mother is honorable, worthy, and like no other gift this earth contains. Just as Mary birthed Jesus, we have the privilege of birthing great grace. And as we do, we see His beauty and love chase after us in every circumstance, whether it is a challenge or a blessing. There will be plenty of both, difficult days and suffering, but there will be beauty unending and memories forever.

Memorize verse 6 today. Light a candle, and delight in the presence of God you've experienced this week.

A Simple Prayer

*Jesus, Your beauty and love chase after me
every day of my life. I am back home in Your house
for the rest of my life.*

Forgiveness

"I'm living outrageously loved—and that jolly well settles it." A British man named Graham Cooke said that.

I certainly have felt that since having children. It is amazing how the gift of a new baby can make us feel loved even in the midst of a lack of sleep and exhausted bodies and . . . and . . . and. There is a certain ecstasy with children; they are the evidence of a miracle.

There is a paradox when you consider the definition of *love*. *Unconditional love* means that there are no limits or conditions; it is complete love. There's no settling when it comes to real love. It always sees the good, and as a result, the not-so-good behavior has a chance to fall by the wayside. It is constantly seeking to encourage, to bring life, and to shut down death. Real love is life.

And we were made for eternal living.

Yes, our human bodies will fail us at some time. But thank God this is not all we have going for us.

Think about this perspective of love, and let's learn the art of forgiveness—which essentially is the art of giving, of generosity, of living outrageously loved. Children are such gifts from God. They birth in us who we were created to be from the very beginning. I love that. Living loved is why we are here. *It's our purpose.*

I love being loved, not because of a false sense of insecurity—though there are surely spots in me that are still in the process of becoming fully secure. I love being loved because that is why God made me. To be cherished. Just like He made you to be cherished. And He fills me to overflow when I give that love away.

This gives life meaning, and it has been my absolute happiest way to grow. No storm can weather our path when we live a life loved. No discipline or correction makes us second-guess ourselves in the heart of God because living a life loved is always about being called higher. From glory to glory. And mothering is always about going lower—but rising in glory.

And so, life is this ebb and flow of glory. Receiving love and then giving it out. And each time, my joy bubble increases and increases. Fear disappears. Forgiveness is innate. Joy tastes good.

We are saved by grace so that none of us can boast about our blessings. They are a gift from God. We are fully accepted into the generous heart of our Father (see Ephesians 2:8; Isaiah 53:3). And when we receive love that way, our motherhood transforms everyone it encounters.

Day 36

And whenever you stand praying, if you have anything against anyone, forgive him, that your Father in heaven may also forgive you your trespasses.

Mark 11:25 NKJV

Out of an inner position of gratitude and abundance, we can give and forgive. Our children are just that: children. We are the ones who teach them how to process, forgive, and respond to circumstances. When our cup is full, we can overflow with wisdom and blessing as an example to them. It is our own inner journey that provides us the means to give to our children well. Though we will always make mistakes (after all, we are human), it is in the process of forgiveness that we can work through old cycles, hurtful words or actions, and failures.

Children are some of the most forgiving and resilient people on the planet. Even though everything will not always go as planned, we can always communicate through hard circumstances in order to come up with better solutions. The essence of motherhood is forgiveness: to give in advance. We give our family love because He first loved us.

Brainstorm a few ways that you can give in advance to your family today. Perhaps wake a little early and prepare the coffee pot for you and your husband. Think through your child's favorite games and play them whenever asked. Make a favorite sweet treat or go out for ice cream if possible. What are a few simple gestures that would show them how much you care for them?

A Simple Prayer

Jesus, thank You for Your forgiveness.

Thank You for giving to me in advance. Help me to receive

Your grace and give it to others.

Day 37

Praise the Lord! Oh, give thanks to the Lord,
for He is good! For His mercy endures forever.

Psalm 106:1 NKJV

Forgiveness is an act of giving, listening, nurturing, setting boundaries, and letting go. It is a pattern that creates both roots and wings. When we are the ones who make the mistake, it is important as parents to learn how our actions made our children feel. Listening has so much power to heal. When a child can be expressive enough to share his or her feelings and thoughts, it gives way to openness and forgiveness. An apology from a parent can go an extremely long way! At the same time, it is also appropriate to set a boundary for when feelings seem to go overboard or become counterproductive. If there is room for an honest assessment but also a boundary for proper guidance, forgiveness can make its way into hearts.

As parents, we will have a lot of opportunities for growth, self-control, and grace. Likewise, when a child does something wrong, it is just as important to walk through the process with them (and that often depends on the age of the child). The first several years of parenting seem to focus more on parental forgiveness, sleepless nights, and a lot of expended energy. We are then granted the opportunities to pay it forward!

What are some ways that you can remain more self-aware when listening to your kids? In what areas do proper boundaries need to be set? What are some things that perhaps just need to be let go?

A Simple Prayer

Jesus, give me ears to listen and wisdom to share.

Let me always have a heart of humility so that

forgiveness can reign in me as a lifestyle.

Day 38

You will tell his people how to be saved through the forgiveness of their sins.

Luke 1:77 CEB

Forgiveness responds, not reacts. When in doubt, it is good to take a quiet stance. Refuse to give back frustration in words, in haste, or in argument. Settle yourself before trying to engage in a difficult situation. It is often best to give time for inside work before addressing anything that feels out of your control. The responsibility of a mother is often high, but it can be handled with grace. We often will feel overwhelmed, overextended, and stretched beyond our capacity. It is the nature of the job! But before reacting, even if we have the right to react, it is always more gratifying to choose a minute to breathe, reset our focus, and then respond. Forgiveness is often as simple as that. We can choose not to destructively react, even though we could. We can remember that our children are still learning and that they learn by our example. Many times we are frustrated not because they have done anything wrong, but simply because it takes a lot of energy to teach all the time. Motherhood is the toughest yet best job around. When we can focus on reality, it helps us take daily hiccups into a proper perspective.

What are your most triggering situations with your children? When they do not listen? When they get messy? During temper tantrums? Try taking a quiet stance before reacting in any of these situations. Try to understand, breathe, and respond with love.

A Simple Prayer

Jesus, please grant me the patience I need to be a loving parent. Help me to pause and to listen before I make a response. Help me to always choose love.

Day 39

*Since I know, my God, that you examine the mind
and take delight in honesty, I have freely given all these
things with the highest of motives.*

1 Chronicles 29:17a CEB

Honesty is the key to forgiveness. Parenting thrives on authenticity and communication. When we are honest with our feelings in a healthy manner, our kids will also be honest with theirs. One of the most important tools for mothering is communication. When we learn how to listen and how to respond to one another, there is no obstacle or situation that cannot be supported and transformed into an opportunity for growth. Stress is most often caused because of a lack of expression. When we give expression to our hurt or frustration, we honor ourselves. We release what is trapped inside. And when we can share this with our children, they get to see a healthy example of authentic self-care. They reflect our example! We set the stage for them to be able to have their own processes while also assuring them we will be there for support. Authentic communication is the key to true forgiveness and healthy interactions as a family.

Practice listening. Practice self-awareness and honesty. Practice expressing yourself in a healthy way. This can start privately by keeping a journal, talking with an adult friend, or even talking with your child. Look for ways to learn how to communicate effectively. It will grow your relationship for years to come!

A Simple Prayer

Jesus, give me the courage to be honest with myself.

Help me to foster my authenticity though it may seem new

and uncomfortable. Help me to lead with forgiveness.

Day 40

Jesus called the children to him and said,
"Let the little children come to me, and do not hinder them, for
the kingdom of God belongs to such as these. Truly I tell you,
anyone who will not receive the kingdom of God like a little
child will never enter it."

Luke 18:16–17 NIV

We made it! A journey through identity, expectations, grief, self-care, comparison, self-acceptance, presence, and forgiveness all intertwined in the life of a mother. There is so much to be grateful for as we embark on this adventure of parenting, loving, and giving. It truly is a gift; it comes with great challenges and great rewards. There really is nothing else like it. As life continues to propel us forward, remember that the little things are the big things—and there is joy to be found in it all! Take a moment today to celebrate. You are a great mother; you took time out to experience this journey because you care. You care about the well-being of yourself and of your family. Yes, you will make mistakes. But you also will have honest conversation, nurturing of wounds, a lot of forgiveness, and even more joy.

Take a few minutes to write a gratitude list. During the course of the day, continue to add all the things you are thankful for to your list. At the end of the day, read them out loud. This is the beginning of a newfound season of joy! And always remember that motherhood is a journey, so repeat this devotional as often as you want. Each season will carry its own lessons, and you can weave these forty days into your life again and again as you plunge through new heights and new depths as a mother.

So when in doubt, just repeat!

A Simple Prayer

Thank You, Jesus! I am grateful for your nurture, care, and grace over my life. Help me to be the best mother I can be, continually to accept Your mercies with each new morning, and to live a life to the fullest for Your glory, myself, and my family.

Special Note

David Humphrey

This endnote is a short recommendation for this book; it is important to have this. You see, if someone is going to write a recommendation for a book, it's important that said person can vouch for the author's credibility on the subject matter that is neatly crafted and awaiting for you on the previous pages. It is one person's way to say, "Hey, everybody, you should read this! It's going to be huge, monumental, and dare I say—life-changing. And I know this to be true because I actually know this person. What this person says is from her heart, and you can trust it." Every good book with a strong message should have recommendations, especially if you want the book to be credible.

And in this case it is a little different. Not only do I know this person, I am married to her. How's that for credibility?

40 Days to a Joyful Motherhood is a journey on motherhood. On the outer appearance, it looks and feels like a devotional that you can walk through yourself, get comfy with, and partake in while on your own journey. And it is. Yet underneath, it comes from a place where the good, the bad, and the messy have surfaced; the sweat, the stains, and the tears of sorrow and even gladness are present; the breakthroughs, the overcoming, the small victories are won. It is a place where all moms can relate.

As a dad and as a husband, I recognize that God has wired me a certain way to provide for my family. To be the steady, wise, and strong voice. To be the leader who keeps our family compass heading north—with my crew in line, ready, and confident to go into the battles of life, no matter how bright or challenging it may be. I am here to kiss scraped knees, bumps, and bruises and to give assurance and encouragement. I am also here to be present—with my time and with my support.

But I also see that as a dad and husband, I'm highly flawed and ill-equipped to complete the job. I lack certain qualities that only a mom and wife can provide. And I am so thankful that Sarah is very equipped to complete the job for our family. Not only has God wired her with certain attributes that make her gentle, warm, and approachable for each of our children, she is in the thick of it daily. She lives it. So it is not only in her DNA, but she has gone through the basic training and is now on the front lines. She has not won all the battles of motherhood (yet), but she is sweeping through it, capturing one small victory at a time. You can say that there is a lot of "pressing through" in our house.

When I sit back and watch Sarah do something that only a mother knows how to do for our Ella, Lucy, and Oliver, I know she did not learn these things from any one book, blog, or conversation from another mom at a park. I know she does these